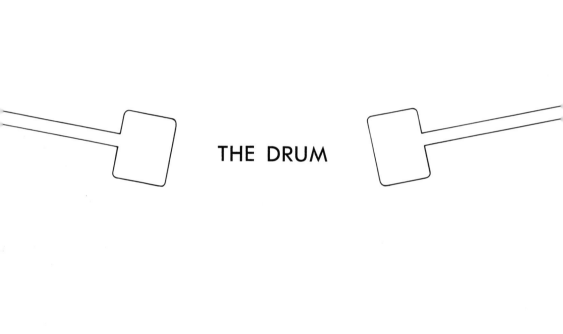

THE DRUM

AN INTRODUCTION
TO THE INSTRUMENT
BY THOMAS A. HILL

THE
DRUM

A KEYNOTE BOOK
FRANKLIN WATTS
NEW YORK

Frontispiece: The Drummer (1926) by Juan Gris,
collection of Baron Gourgaud. New York Public Library.

Library of Congress Cataloging in Publication Data

Hill, Thomas A
  The drum.

  (A Keynote book)
  SUMMARY: An introduction to the drum including
discussions of its construction and use in various
societies, time periods, and kinds of music.
  Bibliography: p.
  1. Drum—Juvenile literature. [1. Drum] I. Title.
ML1035.H54   789'.1'09   74-10694
ISBN 0-531-02789-9

CONTENTS

KEYNOTE
BOOKS

By Bill Ballantine
The Piano
The Flute
The Violin

By Thomas A. Hill
The Guitar
The Drum

Forthcoming titles
The Clarinet
The Trumpet
The Saxophone
The Cello
The Trombone
The Oboe
The Viola

Acknowledgement

I am deeply grateful to
Jim Chapin, who knows much more
about drums than I do, for
help and clarification,
especially on the subject of jazz.

To Knox Burger,
Kitty Sprague,
and Elaine Markson —
three of the world's
good and patient people.

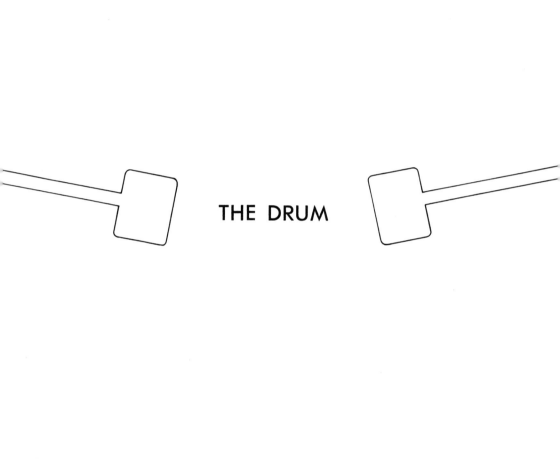

THE DRUM

PRELUDE:
THE UNIVERSAL
DRUM

Rhythm is universal. It is everywhere. From the chirping of crickets to the clopping of a horse's hooves, rhythm is as basic as life — more basic, actually, since even if there were no life there would still be waves lapping steadily at every shore on earth. It is hardly surprising, therefore, that some form of drum can be found in nearly every society on the planet. The Vedda of Ceylon (now Sri Lanka) are the only known culture without drums, and they do a lot of stamping and clapping.

It may be safe to say that the drum, or at least some contrivance intended for the generation of periodic, rhythmic sounds, is the oldest, most basic instrument known to man. Perhaps some caveman, trying to flush a rabbit out of a hollow log, pounded

on the log and received the shock of his life when a deep, booming sound came pounding back. Having no grasp on the principles of *acoustics*, the science of sound, he would find that incredible noise utterly beyond his comprehension. And since people have a tendency to attribute things that they don't understand to spirits or gods, we find that the early history of the drum is linked in nearly every society with the early history of that society's religion. Drums have always had a mystical, supernatural significance to many people; in some cultures today the drummer is revered as a priest or perhaps even a god himself. Drums are played at births, weddings, and funerals. They are played prior to a hunt, during a hunt, after the successful completion of a hunt. Drums are used to ward off evil and to bring good fortune. They are used to heal the sick and to visit plagues upon one's enemies. Now and then, they are simply used to make music.

Since the sound of the drum is mystical and important, so too is the drum. In many societies, the making of a drum is a religious occasion in itself — shrouded in mystery, steeped in ceremony, conducted with reverence and wonder. Every step of the ritualistic process has some mystical meaning. Sacrifices are made to a tree that has been chosen to become a drum. Some cultures feel that any drum seen by a woman before it is completed must be destroyed.

In such drum-worshiping societies, not just anyone can have a drum. The makers and owners of drums are the medicine men, priests, and monarchs. In some cultures, nobody may own a drum but the king, who doesn't even leave his lodging without a retinue of drummers who keep up an incessant tattoo while singing his praises. Showing disrespect for a drum in such a culture can be as bad as desecrating a flag in the Western part of the world — worse, in fact, because desecrating a flag brings only disapproval and perhaps a fine with a few days in jail. Stick

A call to arms on an
early African war drum

(5)

your tongue out at a drum in some parts of the world, and you're asking to be struck by lightning.

Ironically, in the West, where music has taken many sophisticated and difficult forms that challenge the very limits of a drummer's skill, drummers tend to be underrated. Although the drum is indisputably a vital part of nearly every form of music known to man, the person who plays drums in the West is seldom revered.

But there is a great deal more to being a drummer than pounding on a membrane four times per measure. Despite the fact that the function of the drum is indeed very basic in many cultures, we find that in other parts of the world it takes on a baffling intricacy. The heavily improvisational music of India, for example, involves over four hundred basic rhythm structures, and it is understood over there that it can take even the most skillful drummer a lifetime to master them all. Try playing any instrument as fast as you can — in, say, 17/4 time — and you will better appreciate the effort necessary to master the art and skill of Indian drumming.

If you lean toward rock music, listen to *Toad*, the dazzling drum solo recorded by Ginger Baker with the rock group Cream. If you prefer jazz, try to imagine how much less exciting jazz would be if it were deprived of the legacies of Gene Krupa, Elvin Jones, Chick Webb, Buddy Rich, and Max Roach. And if classical music is your first love, listen to — or better still, observe a performance of — Béla Bartók's *Concerto for Two Pianos, Percussion, and Orchestra*. This piece of music — which keeps two percussionists constantly busy on three timpani, two side drums, bass drum, cymbal, suspended cymbal, *tam-tam*, triangle, and

This Indonesian drummer,
also the town mayor,
is conducting a special sort
of symphony brought by
musicians from another village.

xylophone — will help you to understand that, as far as the symphony orchestra is concerned, there is no such thing as a mere drummer. There is the percussionist, and he is a highly trained, master musician, upon whose talents the most strenuous demands are continuously being made. Any percussionist who survives a performance of Bartók's composition will realize this as he takes his third curtain call along with the pianist.

This book won't teach you to be a master drummer. But hopefully it will help you to develop a historical perspective on the instrument, will help you to understand where drums came from, and how they got from there to where they are today. Mastering the drums, like mastering anything, is ultimately the responsibility of the person doing the mastering. Drums can easily be a worthy challenge to the most musically gifted.

A war song by
Wichita Indians in 1905

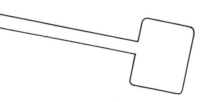

SO WHAT
IS A
DRUM?

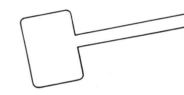

Before getting too far into a book on drums, we really should define what it is we're talking about.

Musical instruments are divided into groups, or families — strings, woodwinds, brass, percussion — on the basis of how they produce sound or of what they are generally made. The percussion instruments are those that produce sound through some kind of striking — either the instrument itself is struck, or it involves parts that strike or scrape against one another. Obviously, the drum is a percussion instrument, as are the xylophone, cymbal, triangle, glockenspiel, *Turkish crescent*, woodblock, and castanets.

Did you know, by the way, that the piano is a percussion instrument? This is because it produces sound by means of felt-tipped hammers that strike

Early Chinese war drums called nacaras
by Marco Polo. They were immense
kettle drums shaped like brass cauldrons
tapering to the bottom and covered with
dried buffalo hide that had been scraped
and tightly stretched for the drum-head.

against wire strings. The designation is more than a technicality; in the orchestra, the piano is classified with the percussion.

As for the percussion instruments that remain when the piano is moved aside, they are divided into two subgroups, *idiophones* and *membranophones*. Idiophones are those instruments made of materials that are sonorous, or sound-producing, without essential modification. Castanets, rattles, and gourds are idiophones, because they don't need help from anybody to be sonorous. The triangle is an idiophone, as are the cymbal and the woodblock.

Membranophones are those instruments that produce sound because something that is not naturally sonorous has been modified so that it is. Specifically, they are the instruments that involve a tightened membrane of some sort, stretched over a shell, bowl, or frame. The frame serves two purposes: it keeps the membrane tight, so that it will vibrate fast enough to produce an audible and potentially musical sound, and it acts as a resonator, to deepen or amplify the sound that results.

Drums are membranophones.

Have you ever wondered why drums sound the way they do? Why, when you pound on a kettledrum, do you get a sound that can be heard for blocks?

To answer that, we have to get into the science of acoustics which examines the properties of sound. Basically, sound is vibration: hit something, and the impact produces sound waves, oscillations, that move through the air and to the inner ear. This causes elements of the inner ear to vibrate, and it is this vibration that the brain interprets as sound.

When you hit the membrane (or *vellum*) of a drum, it vibrates. This causes the air around it to vibrate. Now, if you can confine

Nigerian singers use these calabash
gourds to produce two different
sounds — one with seeds inside and the
other with a net of beads outside.

(13)

*The snare drum was used
mainly for military purposes
as seen in this lithograph
of the Civil War period.*

that air, keep that shock wave from rippling quietly off into oblivion, the sound will be intensified. If you confine that air with a resonant material, the vibrating air will cause that material to vibrate, and the sound will be intensified even further.

That is how a drum works. Some sort of thin material is stretched — tightly enough that it will vibrate rapidly — over a shell made of resonant material, and that shell confines a column of air. The interaction of membrane, shell, and air column produces that sound we talked about — the one you can hear for blocks.

There are three basic types of drums. There are single-membrane drums that are open at one end, drums with a membrane at each end, and drums with a single membrane over a sort of bowl. Examples of the three types would be bongos, the snare drum, and the kettledrum, respectively.

There are many uses to which drums are put, and each of these different basic types lends itself to different uses. A kettledrum would usually be inappropriate in a jazz band, and bongos have no business in Beethoven's Ninth Symphony.

Having substantially determined what constitutes a drum, perhaps it is time to determine — or at least to conjecture about — how drums originated, where they came from, and why.

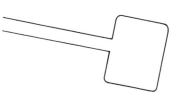

THE DRUM
IN AFRICA

Since there are drums just about everywhere there
are people, and apparently have been for as long
as people have been leaving records (however fragmentary) of their civilizations, tracking the drum
down to one point of origin is not only an impossible
task, it's a misguided one. No single place, no one
culture, invented the drum. The drum dates back to
prehistory everywhere you look. Clay drums exca-
vated in Moravia date back to 6,000 B.C. Meso-
potamian sculptures from five thousand years ago
feature drums, as do monuments and paintings of
comparable antiquity from ancient Egypt, Persia,
Assyria, India, and China. South American Indian
cultures prior to the rise of the Aztecs and Incas had
drums — thousands of years before Cortez.

A rock painting from South Africa.
Notice the ornamented drum.

We must be content in assuming that at some point in every cradle of civilization, somebody hit something, liked the sound, and decided to hit it again.

Although we might thus be tempted to choose a starting point by stabbing a finger at a spinning globe with both eyes closed, there is one starting point that is better than others, and that is Africa. Drums have played a rich and varied role in the history of Africa, and there remain many places there where instruments are still being made as they were hundreds, even thousands, of years ago. Furthermore, many African rhythms and attitudes have become established in "Western" music through such music as jazz and the blues.

Since the histories of the drum in Japan or Siberia — interesting and well-documented though they may be — would not directly relate to any music with which we are familiar, Africa makes the most sense. The natives of our own continent have been playing drums for centuries, too, but you never hear their music on the radio.

Perhaps the most basic instrument to be found anywhere is simply "the drum of the earth." Tribes in Ethiopia dig two holes of different depth in the ground, and pound on the inner walls of these holes with the palms of their hands. The drum of the earth is found throughout Africa, and has been used in all parts of the continent throughout history.

The day that man first got beyond holes in the ground may have been the day our rabbit-hunter, having long since forgotten the rabbit, came traipsing back to camp with his hollow log in tow. He showed everybody what hollow logs were good for, and it wasn't long before this mysterious and unexplained sound came to be regarded as the voice of a god. In nearly every prim-

*This tribe in Burma is
playing its war drum — a large,
hollowed out tree-trunk.*

Beautifully carved Mayan slit drums

itive society on earth, the drum is looked upon with reverence, and not infrequently with fear.

So they pounded on hollow logs for awhile, back there in pre-historic days. Then one day it occurred to somebody that when there is a shortage of hollow logs, nobody is stopping you from hollowing out your own. This realization introduced the element of creativity into the world of the drum, and hastened the development not only of the drum itself, but of its role in the many cultures of Africa.

The first carved drums, or slit drums, were very basic — perhaps because of the simplicity of available tools. A slit was carved into the entire length of a large log, and this slit served as a resonating chamber. These first log drums were huge; there is a Sudanese drum in the British Museum that is nine feet long, and there are stories of drums as long as forty feet.

As might be expected, the sound made by these drums had considerable carrying power, and this led to the development of new uses for drums — most obviously, communication. Early European explorers were frequently baffled to learn, as they thrashed through unexplored jungle, that the tribes they encountered were obviously expecting them. Their presence had been announced by "bush telegraph." Using codes that developed over the years the complexity of human speech, the tribes of Africa learned to send with drum signals everything from news of advancing Englishmen to weather reports. John F. Carrington[1] tells of watching a man beat out a brief message on a drum, and asking him what the message was. The drummer replied that he was out of cigarettes, and had asked a friend in a nearby village to bring him a pack.

Though the range of any given drum might only be a few miles, a message could be relayed over considerable distance in a very short time, by means of a series of drums. Since the use of

1 Carrington, John F. "The Talking Drums of Africa," *Scientific American,* December, 1971.

drums as a means of communication is common to most African tribes — though it is dying out under the relentless onslaught of "civilization" — there are about as many drum codes or languages as there are tribes. This isn't the obstacle to intertribal communication that it might seem to be; since marriage between people of different tribes is widespread, there's usually an interpreter around.

A phenomenon known as *sympathetic vibration* added another element to the mystique of drums. Anyone who has spent a good deal of time around musical instruments knows that many instruments will respond to certain vibrations in their vicinity by emitting vibrations of their own — whether anybody is playing them or not. Imagine the effect it must have had the first time somebody said something and a nearby drum talked back. A man who really got the hang of it could appear to be conversing with a drum. The witch doctors and medicine men, always ready to demonstrate their affiliation with higher powers, were quick to see the possibilities in this, and soon the drum (whose long slit was already suspected of being the residence of assorted gods and the spirits of deceased relatives) was shrouded in even more ritual, mystery, and supernatural fanfare.

Since faith is a powerful force in any society, drums became highly effective instruments of medicine and magic. A man who could convince his fellows that he controlled the power of the drum could inflict actual pain and cure actual disease just by declaring that he was doing so. With the medicine men getting excellent results, it wasn't long before drums were being asked to lend their influence to everything from rainmaking to increasing the prospects for victory in territorial disputes. This explains the existence and importance of rain dances, war dances, and the

A small cylindrical hand drum from Melanesia that was cut from a solid block of wood and whitened with lime in the carvings.

(22)

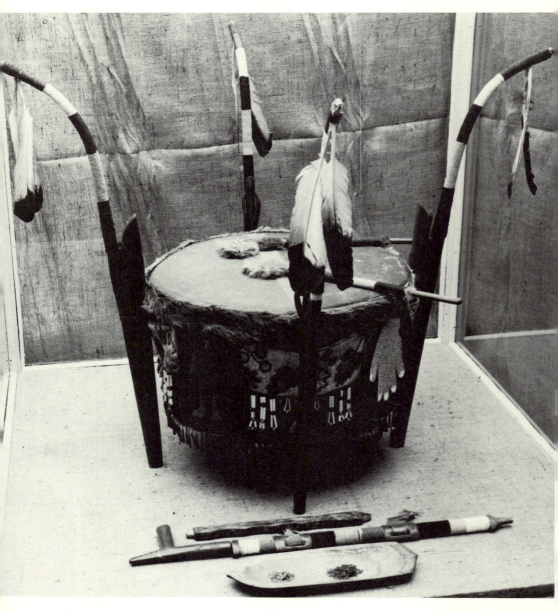

Above: an Indian dream dance drum.
Left: an elaborate Japanese O'Daiko drum on a stand.
Right: a carved and painted drum from French Congo.

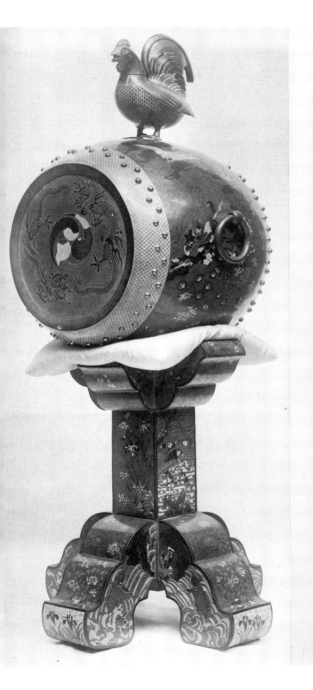

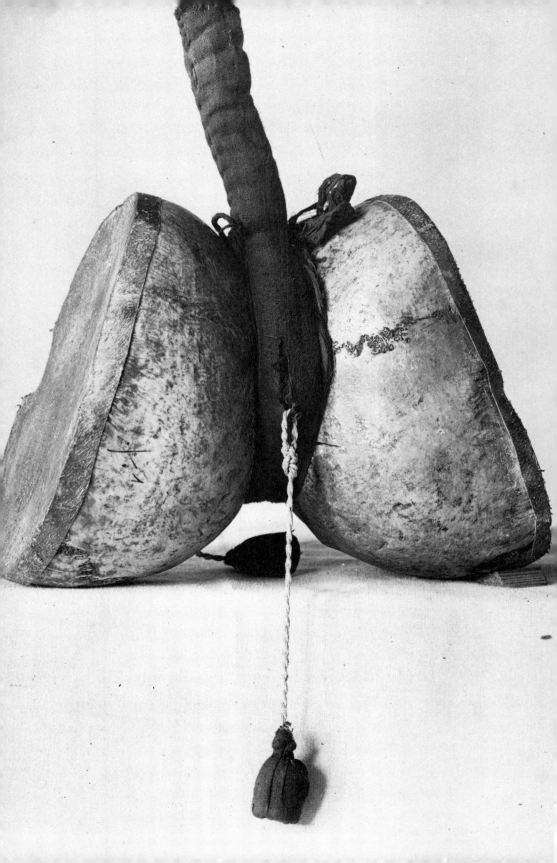

like, and it explains why drums are always involved in such rituals. The drum serves as more than mere accompaniment; having the voice of a god, it is believed to bring the presence of that god into the ritual. The drum is a telephone to the gods, if you will, transmitting their power to mortals.

Once the supernatural element was thoroughly interwoven into the business of making and playing drums, people began embellishing their drums with decorations. The decorations served to define the purpose of the drum, and besides, an impressive-looking drum just might be better at prodding a god into action than an unimpressive one. And so, many of the log drums, early and contemporary (for they are still made and used) are elaborately carved and painted. Some are carved in the fancied image of the god or spirit they are meant to represent, some in the form of totems that tell stories, some simply with hunting scenes and the like.

Clearly, the drum has long been an integral part of the affairs of human beings. It was integral before it even looked like what we think of as a drum. So when did it start to look like a drum?

To answer that question, we have to go back to the drum of the earth, and the discovery of membranes.

Even after the slit drum had come along, the drum of the earth remained important — because of the importance of the earth itself. Playing music on the earth was not a practice to be abandoned just because somebody had invented a drum that was portable. No, the drum of the earth continued to be used, and led to some interesting discoveries itself.

The major discovery might have been accidental. Somebody may have had an animal hide that needed drying. Perhaps, hoping that improved air circulation might speed up the drying process, they stretched the hide over a hole, pegging down the corners to keep them from curling up. The hide dried, shrank,

In India skull drums such as this one were used in temples.

(27)

Reconstructed clay drums with
animal-hide vellums, dating from
about 2000 B.C. in Bohemia

tightened up. And then, when it was time to remove it, somebody accidentally gave it a tap and was rewarded with a hearty B-flat. Lending credence to such a theory is the existence of the Bantu *ingqongqo*, a drum that consists only of a hide stretched between two poles and beaten with sticks.

The practice of placing boards or planks over a hole and stamping on them has been common throughout Africa for centuries; this, too, might have been an early ancestor of the membrane drum.

When the first actual membranophone — a hollow vessel with a hide secured tightly over an opening — was made is as lost in antiquity as the rest, but there are clay drums with animal-hide vellums in the National Museum in Prague that date back over three thousand years. The earliest drumheads, made from the uncured skins of snakes, fish, and lizards, didn't last very long. These early drums were played almost exclusively with the hands; beaters came later, probably at about the same time that drumheads started being made of the tougher hides of cattle and hunted game. Cave paintings, Ethiopian sculptures, and other sources dating back to the eighth century clearly show drums with heads secured with twine.

Arabia (using the word in its broadest sense, to define the entire non-Hebrew, Semitic world) isn't always thought of as a part of Africa, but it covers the entire Northeastern portion of the African continent. The Arabs have played a vital role in the development of Western percussion; it was probably the Arabian and Turkish drums brought back to Europe by the Crusaders during the twelfth century that truly introduced percussion consciousness to a continent that had not previously been particularly interested. Some say that it was the Moors, crossing the Straits of Gibraltar a few centuries earlier, who brought the first really interesting drums with them. This may well be true, and in the absence of conclusive evidence the debate is not likely to be resolved.

Whoever brought them, the first drums to which Europe paid any sustained attention definitely came from Africa.

Having established this vital link, perhaps we should turn our eyes toward Europe to see what those drums were like — and to find out what the Europeans did with them.

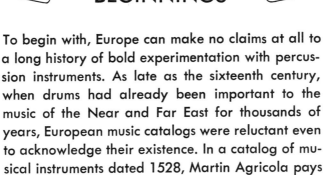

THE DRUM
IN EUROPE:
BEGINNINGS

To begin with, Europe can make no claims at all to a long history of bold experimentation with percussion instruments. As late as the sixteenth century, when drums had already been important to the music of the Near and Far East for thousands of years, European music catalogs were reluctant even to acknowledge their existence. In a catalog of musical instruments dated 1528, Martin Agricola pays close attention to cymbals, bells, xylophone, even anvil, but doesn't mention drums at all.

Whoever brought the first African drums to Europe — whether it was the Crusaders, wandering back from Palestine with their hands full of souvenirs, or the Moors — it was during the thirteenth century that the two most important drums appeared.

The *tabor*, a small, two-headed drum with a *snare* (or strand of gut) on the lower head, and *nakers*, a pair of single-headed, bowl-shaped drums that Turkish cavalry drummers wore at the belt, probably date back before Christ; nothing like them existed in Europe before 1200 or so. Examination of these drums makes it clear that they are the immediate ancestors, respectively, of the modern snare drum and paired kettledrum, or *timpani*. A painting done by Vittore Carpaccio of Venice around 1505 shows a Turkish instrument nearly identical to the modern military side-drum.

Not everybody was impressed. Sebastian Virdung, the eminent German musicologist whose *Musica Getuscht* (published in 1551) remains a valuable source of information on the music and instruments of his time, called drums "rumpelfesser" — which means "rattle-barrels" or "rumbling tubs." "These," said Virdung, "are to the taste of such as cause much unrest to pious old people of the earth. . . . And I verily believe that the devil must have had the making of them, for there is no pleasure or anything good about them."

Such reviews notwithstanding, the tabor was quick to become the most common drum in Europe once it was introduced. England called it the *taberett*. In Germany it was the *tambourin*, in France, the *tambourin* and *taboret*, in Italy, the *tamburino*, and in Spain, the *atambor*. Apparently, there was no standard tabor, although all had two membranes with a snare on the beaten head. The fragmentary evidence available to us suggests that the heads were probably fastened with a network of crossed cords. The head was usually made of sheepskin or calfskin, although the hides of donkeys or even wolves might be used where sheep and calves were in short supply. According to writers of the time, the tabor was usually a foot across the head and two feet deep. Occasionally, there was a snare on both heads. It was always played, evidently, with one stick, and so the rhythms used probably weren't very complex.

Its earliest success was as a military instrument. The Swiss ap-

This painting done by
Fra Angelico during the
early Italian Renaissance
shows an angel holding
a small snare drum.

*An engraving of the Battle of Lexington
in 1775. During the American Revolution,
the drum's significance was greatly enhanced.*

parently came up with the idea of teaming the fife with the drum; first mentioned in Swiss municipal records as early as 1332, this proved to be an enduring combination, being adopted all over Europe — as well as in America, when America was discovered later.

If any music was being written for the drum at this time, little of it has survived; it was probably learned mostly by ear, passed on from one drummer to the next. The only available material is in the form of military instructions — signaling codes, and the like. Thoinot Arbeau's *Orchésographie* (1588) is perhaps the most important such work; in the form of a dialog between a teacher and his pupil, it explains a multitude of rhythms and marching cadences in considerable detail.

When you consider how important communication can be during a battle, the military importance of the drum is easy to understand. Soldiers have to know when to advance, when to hold, when to retreat, and drum signals were an obvious way for field commanders to convey such information to their troops. Military drum codes became quite elaborate, and it was an unfortunate drummer indeed who fell into enemy hands. His captors would be inclined to use whatever means they considered necessary to persuade him to reveal the codes, and torture was common.

Strategic importance gave drummers considerable social status, as well. They were classified as servants of royalty, held officers' ranks, and were entitled to wear the garb of nobility. A drummers' guild, which decided who was permitted to become a drummer and who wasn't, chose candidates from only the most respectable families. Potential drummers were required to serve long apprenticeships, and were only allowed to perform their function after they had been officially declared "freemen."

This elitism probably helps to explain the lack of written drum music from the period; the people who had the information only gave it to people they deemed worthy of it. A nonguild drummer caught playing a drum was punished, and even today timpani cannot be played in London's Guildhall unless royalty is officially present.

It took a little longer for the drum to find its way into non-military contexts — largely due to such sentiments as those expressed by Virdung. Rattle-barrels may be terrific on a battle-field, where presumably you need as much volume as you can get. But as soon as serious music is being discussed — that's a different matter altogether. For one thing, a musical instrument should be something you can play music on, and how much music can you play with a range of one tone — a vague, indistinct tone, at that?

This was definitely a problem. But in the middle of the sixteenth century there was a major development in the technology of drum making that changed everything. Nobody seems to know who put the first ones into production, but paintings of the period begin to show drums — specifically, kettledrums — on which the heads are not laced or tacked to the bowl but are fastened by means of screw mechanisms that can be loosened or tightened. With the development of *screw-tensioning*, different tones could be played on one drum, with some degree of control, for the first time.

The idea itself wasn't new; Leonardo da Vinci, who foresaw everything from helicopters to submarines, mentioned screw-tightened drums in his notebooks around 1490. But he never got around to manufacturing one. (He didn't make any helicopters, either.)

So, according to Hans Burgkmair's *The Skill of Music*, published in 1550, German manufacturers were soon producing screw-tensioned timpani in some quantity, and these were finding their way into symphony orchestras. The number of screws were as few as five or as many as eight, with the earlier drums generally having more. There wasn't any standard size, either; the early screw-tensioned drums measured anywhere between seventeen and twenty-eight inches across. (The modern standard for a pair of timpani is twenty-five and twenty-eight

In this contemporary cartoon of Napoleon
"throwing sand into the eyes of the masses,"
notice the royal garb of the drummer.

inches.) They always appeared in pairs, though — following the Turkish example — and the usual difference in diameter between the two drums in a pair was about two inches.

These early drums were generally tuned in *intervals* — the differences in pitch between two notes or tones — of a fourth (five halftones apart on a *chromatic scale* which progresses in twelve, evenly spaced halftones). The higher-pitched drum was generally tuned to D and the lower to A. As an indication of how attitudes about the drum began to improve, it was at about this time that composers first began to write drum parts into their music with some consistency — Jean Baptiste Lully, Johann Sebastian Bach, and Henry Purcell being among the first to do so.

Credit for the first orchestral use of kettledrums generally is given to Lully, born in 1633, whose opera *Thesée* featured them in 1675. Matthew Locke's opera *Psyche*, written at about the same time, calls for the use of drums, but the written parts have been lost. In France, drum parts (albeit military ones) had already been written by the brothers Philidor, musicians of the court of Louis XIV.

Bablon's *Marches de Timbales pour les Gardes du Roi*, published in 1705, is a military composition, but it is worth mentioning here because it features the first known instance of two drums, tuned to different pitches, being struck at the same time to produce a chord — a device widely believed to have been used first by Ludwig van Beethoven in his Ninth Symphony.

The works of Bach, Lully, Pascal Colasse, Purcell, Orazio Benevoli, and Pavel Josef Vejnavosky demonstrate that drums were firmly established in the symphony orchestra by the end of the seventeenth century.

These first orchestral kettledrums were crude by today's standards. Keeping an even tension on a drumhead that had to be controlled with several individually-turned screws was impossible, and tone quality often suffered dismally. Furthermore, even the best drummer needed some time to retune his drum before being ready to produce a different tone, and over the din of the orchestra it wasn't always possible to know whether he had everything adjusted properly. Nobody could know until he struck the drum, and if it wasn't the right tone — well, it was just too late.

As a result, the seventeenth-century composers were cautious in their use of timpani, very seldom requiring a change of tuning in the middle of a work. And if they did write in a change, they also wrote in a good, long pause in the part, so that the drummer would have all the time he needed to make his adjustments.

Drums don't appear much in written records again until around 1730, although pictorial evidence assures us that they were very much in use, not only in orchestras but in the church and theater as well. A print in the *Leipzig Hymnbook*, published in 1710, shows Johann Kuhnau (Bach's predecessor as organist at St. Thomas) conducting an ensemble of organ, trumpet, strings, and pair of kettledrums.

Bach was probably the first to conduct lavish experiments with drums, although he always stayed with a single pair and never called upon them to change key in the middle of a piece. If a piece of music changed key, the drums fell silent until the original key had returned.

(Part of Bach's problem might have been that there were apparently only two kettledrums in Leipzig at the time, and they were jointly owned by two churches. You can't play music on three instruments when there are only two in town.)

As for George Frederick Handel, to whose frequently thunderous choral music the timpani often lent their authority, his use of drums was consistent, but never really experimental.

In the middle of the eighteenth century, three compositions were performed that mark a significant step forward. Francesco Barsanti's *Concerto Groos* (1743) calls for timpani to be played in three keys, the first known composition to do so. Since we know of no technological advances to account for this — kettledrums were still adjusted with individually-turned screws — Barsanti's timpanist was presumably kept busy during pauses.

*The drum's importance in military events is
again illustrated in this drawing of
Nathan Hale's execution, which took place in 1776.*

In addition, Johann Melchior Molter and J. W. Hertel produced a flurry of compositions around 1750 calling for timpani to be played in three keys. Hertel, incidentally, even wrote a piece that called for the use of ten kettledrums, to be played by a single player. The drummer who rose to this task was apparently equal to it, for not only did he get to the right drum at the right time, he performed acrobatic feats with his drumsticks as he ran from one drum to the next. The man's name has been forgotten, unfortunately.

Around the middle of the eighteenth century, Europe was swept by a musical fad involving the military music of Turkey. As military music, it was bound to rely heavily on percussion; the Turkish military bands, called *Jannisary* bands, were about as percussive as they come. (A *Janizary* was an infantryman in the Turkish army.) A Jannisary band might include several bass drums and kettledrums. If there was anyone in Europe who had managed to avoid percussion before, Jannisary music soon took care of them.

Not much more was heard from the kettledrum until Franz Joseph Haydn began receiving acclaim toward the end of the century. Haydn was fond of drums; he had started playing them as a child, and was himself a virtuoso. His writing for timpani is distinguished by a high degree of imagination, as well as an obvious understanding of the limitations and strengths of percussion. He scored timpani parts in more than one key; in *The Creation* (1799), the timpani are required to change key several times. As timpani were still tuned by individually-turned screws, such works clearly demanded the services of an excellent timpanist.

Although the fortunes of the drum had definitely risen since the time of Sebastian Virdung, it wasn't until Ludwig van Beethoven achieved prominence that drums really came into their own, and established themselves in the minds of nearly everybody as more than rumbling tubs. The first composer to exploit fully the potential of kettledrums, Beethoven introduced some radical departures from tradition. Although he limited himself to a single pair of timpani, he occasionally used them as a solo instrument. While most other composers kept their timpani tuned in intervals of a fourth or fifth (with the exception of an infrequent, cautious experiment), Beethoven used diminished fifths, minor sixths, and octaves. It should be noted that the works in which he did so are not regarded today as mere curiosities; such innovations occur repeatedly in the works that are regarded as his masterpieces — notably, as mentioned before, his Ninth Symphony. It is interesting, considering his willingness to try new things, that he only wrote one piece in which the drums changed key — the *Missa Solemnis.*

Obviously, technical limitations were bound to impose musical limitations; many brilliant works are occasionally jarred by garish *dissonances* — unharmonious combinations of tones — that puzzle present-day musicologists. Perhaps the most satisfactory explanation for the appearance of what seems to be the wrong note in the work of a master would be that the instruments at his disposal were incapable of playing the right one.

This confronts the modern conductor with a dilemma. There is a great deal of controversy over the question of whether a conductor is best doing his job if he conducts the music as it is written, or if he changes these "wrong" notes to notes that the composer presumably would have used if his drums had been better. The debate shows no signs of subsiding, and it is an intriguing question.

With the beginning of the nineteenth century, the demands that composers were starting to make of drums and the people who played them led to an era of vigorous experimentation with

Ludwig van Beethoven, one of the first composers to fully utilize the potential of kettledrums, offered some radical departures from traditional music.

*A pair of early kettledrums, with
hand-turned cranks, from the 1800s*

machinery — machinery that would enable timpani to be tuned faster, and with some precision. It just wasn't practical to fill up a stage or orchestra pit with kettledrums, and drum makers began to address themselves to the problem.

In 1812 they started getting results. Working in Munich, Gerhard Cramer devised a kettledrum with a hand-turned crank, by means of which all of the screws could be tightened at once. The obvious advantages of Cramer's drum made it a resounding success, but it wasn't long before the competition began coming up with other ideas.

In 1821 Stumpf of Amsterdam invented a drum on which the tension of the head could be varied by rotating the bowl itself — clockwise to tighten it, counterclockwise to loosen it. At the same time, in Germany, Eiblinger fashioned a drum with a movable, internal hoop that did basically the same thing. And in 1837 Cornelius Ward of London devised a drum on which the tension was controlled by a system of cables and pulleys.

All of these involved hand-tuning of some kind, and their common disadvantage was difficulty in keeping an even tension on the head. Uneven tension resulted in poor tonal quality, even though ease of tuning was improved considerably.

The first timpani operated with foot-pedals seem to have appeared in Germany around 1843. These drums made use of a different principle entirely; instead of altering pitch by varying the tension on the head, they contained three concentric steel rings that could be pressed against the underside of the membrane, thus enlarging or decreasing the area of the head that actually vibrated. This changed the frequency of vibration, which changed the pitch. Each ring operated independently.

Many drums of this type were eventually produced, some having as many as seven rings and pedals. The main disadvantage of this system seems to have been the cumbersome mechanism involved. The pedal action was very noisy — an obvious problem during quiet pieces of music.

In 1855 Adolphe Sax (the imaginative man who invented the

saxophone) devised a fascinating if short-lived drum that didn't do anything to the membrane to change pitch. Sax's drum changed pitch by means of foot-operated shutters that changed the volume of the confined air column. This drum failed to generate much excitement— perhaps because the mechanism was as noisy as previous ones.

Sax, incidentally, was of the opinion that the shell or bowl of a kettledrum had nothing to do with tone quality, and he produced some kettledrums that didn't have bowls at all. They looked sort of like huge tambourines, without rattles. They didn't prove any more successful than his shutter-operated ones.

By the late 1850s the best kettledrums were being made mostly in Germany and Vienna. Boracci was an eminent drum maker of the time, as were Hudler, Pfundt, and Schneller, all of Vienna. Stumpf, the Dutch manufacturer who concocted the drum with the rotating bowl, was also a leading manufacturer. Mechanisms were becoming rather complex, although the emphasis was on rapid change of pitch rather than on tone quality. For all of the things that were being tried, the manually-tuned drum remained the most widely used.

In practically every field of art or science, we are occasionally confronted with a single person whose work must be recognized as a major turning point. In examining percussion music, we find that there was indeed a single composer after whom things were irretrievably different from what had gone before. That man is Hector Berlioz.

Berlioz was critical of his predecessors' willingness to stay within the limitations imposed by the presence of only two kettledrums, a custom that was seldom and only briefly defied. He had little regard for the limitations imposed by the realities of economics, too; he envisioned a "dream orchestra" of 467 musicians, of whom 53 would be percussionists. There would be eight pairs of timpani (and ten players), three bass drums, six side drums, four pairs of cymbals, six sets of bells, two large, low-pitched bells, six triangles, and four Turkish crescents.

Pedal timpani

Hector Berlioz changed the
nature of percussion music.

Unfortunately, his casual attitude toward matters of finance was not shared by the people who paid the bills; even in those days the performing arts were a hard-nosed matter of selling tickets, paying the rent, and having a little left over for groceries. Berlioz never got to put his dream orchestra together.

He did occasionally get something approaching it, though; his *Grande Messe des Mortes*, written in 1837, calls for sixteen pairs of timpani and ten players. This work is still performed, though not always with the designated number of drums.

Not that everybody was thrilled by Berlioz and his grandiose visions; his works were often received with pronounced hostility. There is even a story that he once stayed up all night keeping watch over his drums, having heard rumors of a conspiracy to slash the membranes.

The demands made by Berlioz in such works as *Hamlet*, *Instrumentation*, the *Fantastic Symphony*, and *Beatrice and Benedict* made it just about impossible for a drummer to get by with hand-tuned kettledrums. They couldn't be adjusted fast enough.

By the time the works of such composers as Felix Mendelssohn and Robert de Diable began to reflect the influence of Berlioz, percussionists had no choice but to turn to the faster, pedal-tuned drums — a change which hastened their improvement. We can determine by listening to the works of Wagner that well-engineered pedal-tuned drums must have been available by the end of the century; nothing else could have kept up with him.

Obviously, somebody was playing these drums while all this was going on, although it was unheard of for an orchestral percussionist to cultivate the kind of personality cult that surrounds some of today's performing artists. A talented drummer was certainly a feather in the cap of any meticulous conductor, but only as the century drew to a close was anyone beginning to preserve for posterity the names of the prominent drummers.

Pietro Pieranzovini, author of a definitive method for kettledrum, was considered a master of percussion; he wrote music for drums, as well. J.A. Smith may have been the best in Europe

In this picture of President Abraham Lincoln and
his family, one of President Lincoln's sons has a drum
for a toy. By the end of the 1800s, the drum was
appearing in many places other than battlefields.

during the 1870s and 1880s. Others who had all the work they could handle were William Gezink, G. Gordon Cleather, and Samuel W. Geldard. It is a fragmentary record at best, an indication of the way in which percussionists were taken for granted.

As the century ended, the drum had certainly come a long way. The prominence of drummer-boys in virtually every military force on earth had brought the drum to everyone's attention; the American Revolution and the Civil War had reconfirmed its importance. Drums figured prominently in the work of every major composer, and were occasionally permitted to come forward to be featured. The combination of advancing technology and improving esteem were preparing the drum for the challenge of the twentieth century.

And an awesome challenge it would be.

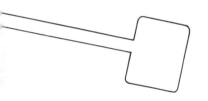

THE TWENTIETH CENTURY

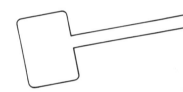

It seems safe to say that the beginning of the 1900s marked a major turning point for music as a whole. As the century began, new and radically different concepts of music began to emerge. Rules, regulations, and beliefs that had been cherished and adhered to for hundreds of years were cast aside, and a whole new musical landscape opened up.

It all began with the dissatisfaction of such figures as Arnold Schoenberg and his pupil Anton Webern with the confines imposed by conventional thinking. Departing from adherence to traditional *tonality*, the harmonic relationships between the tones of a musical scale or system, Schoenberg fashioned a method of composition based on the systematic suspension and avoidance of traditional harmonic re-

Drums had a place in politics
as seen in this picture
of an early bandwagon.

lationships. Schoenberg's creation, which he called *serial music*, differs from chromatically oriented music in that it involves what he termed a "tone row," rather than a melody in the classical sense. In a tone row, each of the twelve tones of the chromatic scale appears once; the tones are arranged in any sequence of the composer's choosing, and all twelve tones must appear before any one can be repeated. The tone row can be reversed, though, or inverted, or reversed and inverted; the number of tones in a nonrepetitive sequence can thus be as many as forty-eight.

It makes a lot more sense to listen to this highly systematized music than to be content with a description. So check the lists for suggested listening in the back of this book.

Much of this new and startlingly different music requires some training and familiarity on the part of the listener; it is frequently dismissed by people who haven't cultivated the understanding necessary to appreciate it fully as baffling and perhaps offensive noise. Hopefully, this slightly highbrow-sounding information won't interfere with your desire to explore the territory; many exciting and lavishly pleasant experiences are somewhat disturbing — or at least puzzling — at first.

In such works as *Five Pieces for Orchestra*, *Gurrelieder*, and *Moses and Aaron* (his last work), Schoenberg was among the first to explore fully the potential of percussion as an indispensable part of the whole tonal and melodic essence of a work. No longer called upon simply to complement and emphasize (however magnificently at times) the more dominant elements defined by other instruments, percussion became with Schoenberg a true part of the system in which those elements unfolded.

Schoenberg's influence was felt by nearly every composer of the day, whether he was serially oriented or not. Everyone began taking full advantage of the percussion section. The music of Sibelius, Mahler, Rachmaninoff, Prokofiev, and Nielsen began to reflect the change; Saint-Saëns's *Samson and Delilah* features a timpani solo (still a rarity), and his *Algerian Suite* is regarded by percussionists as an extremely challenging piece.

Richard Strauss, who perhaps belongs at the end of the romantic era rather than at the beginning of the modern era, found himself aligned chronologically with the serialists, and their influence is evident in his work. *Rosenkavalier, Salome, Elektra, Till Eulenspiegel,* and numerous others constantly use percussion to full advantage. Four timpani are necessary for a great deal of his writing, much of which turned out to be more than two of even the most advanced pedal-tuned drums of the day could handle.

At about this time Charles Ives began to make himself heard in the United States, which was still a newcomer among nations whose music was taken seriously. *A Set of Pieces* contains a section in which the timpani play in 2/4 time while the rest of the orchestra plays the following sequence: 2/4, 6/8, 7/16, 2/4, 6/16, 9/16, 2/4. His compositions, which weren't performed very much at the time, are now highly regarded, and he is considered one of the great American composers.

But it is Igor Stravinsky who is probably considered the modern master of percussion; the news that Stravinsky is on the program will warm the cockles of any percussionist's heart — providing he has a great deal of self-confidence. Stravinsky's feeling for percussion is legendary. His writing is extremely challenging but always within bounds of reason; he was an excellent percussionist himself and had a large private collection of instruments, with which he was careful to ascertain the possibility of playing everything he wrote before turning a work loose on the world. His writing for percussion contains many effects: pathos, suspense, humor — even slapstick. He was one of the few composers who knew how to evoke laughter through the subtle use of percussion.

Notable examples of his writing for percussion are *The Firebird* (1910), *Petrouchka* (1911), and *Le Sacre du Printemps* ("The

Rite of Spring," 1913). As was a great deal of the boldly experimental music of the time, much of Stravinsky's writing (*Petrouchka* being typical in this respect) is strikingly nonlinear; that is, instead of having a clearly defined beginning, middle, climax, and resolution, the music wanders around in an apparently casual fashion, doing all manner of delightful things before arriving at a conclusion that is appropriate but not, necessarily, inevitable.

Percussion figures prominently throughout. *Le Sacre du Printemps* calls for five timpani, bass drum, cymbals, tam-tam, triangle, tambourine, antique cymbals, and rasp.

Perhaps the percussionist's favorite of Stravinsky's compositions is *L'Histoire du Soldat* ("A Soldier's Tale"), a narrative playlet inspired by a cycle of Russian folk tales about the adventures of a deserter from the army whose soul is eventually seized by the devil. At the beginning of the score are Stravinsky's careful instructions for the arrangement of the percussion instruments, which include bass drum, large side drum, small side drum, deep military drum without snare, tambourine, triangle, and cymbal. Interesting to note is the jazz influence; Stravinsky had a flare for jazz (his work has been recorded by such artists as jazz clarinetist Benny Goodman), and *L'Histoire du Soldat* contains syncopated rhythms in such sequences as 4/8, 5/16, 7/16, 8/16.

By the time the twentieth century was in full swing — bringing with it such novelties as world wars, electricity, manned flight, and the theory of relativity — previous assumptions about the order of the universe were in ruins. There was a lot to think about, and composers couldn't get their thoughts down on paper fast enough. The world was confronted by an unprecedented

Born in Russia and later a citizen of France, Igor Stravinsky became known as the master of percussion. His compositions changed the contemporary music scene so greatly that the beginning of the modern era in music can be attributed to his works.

flurry of creativity, much of it too recent for us to develop a dry, historical perspective.

But a few tentative judgments can be made. It looks like the works of Gustav Holst will survive; his *The Planets* (1917) is one of the best and most demanding works for percussion in the orchestral repertoire. Debussy, Ravel, Honegger, Lambert, and Aaron Copland are other names that would spring to the mind of a seasoned percussionist if you asked him what composers make his life interesting.

There is Leos Janácek, whose work is unusual in its consistent demand for large numbers of timpani in extremely high registers.

And there is of course Béla Bartók, whose challenging *Concerto for Two Pianos, Percussion, and Orchestra* was mentioned in the beginning of this book. Bartók directed a great deal of attention to the subtle differences in tonal quality that result when different parts of the drumhead are struck — the center as opposed to the edge, and so forth. He frequently stipulated in the scores of his work exactly which area of the head is to be struck to obtain a particular effect. He occasionally called for cymbals to be played with fingernails, or the edge of a knife blade. Percussionists sometimes meet his requirements for a light touch by playing with knitting needles.

Other twentieth-century composers who used percussion to full advantage were Benjamin Britten (First Symphony, 1959); Jaromir Weinberger (*Schwanda the Bagpiper*, 1927); Arnold Bax (*Tintagel*, 1917); Edgard Varèse whose *Ionisation* was the seminal percussion tour de force of the 1920s; Darius Milhaud; William Russell; Erik Satie; Francis Poulenc; Paul Hindemith. But a mere list of names becomes tedious, a description of the music woefully inadequate. Listen to the music — find out for yourself.

To this day, compositions for unaccompanied drums are quite rare. Among the few works available are Daniel Jones's *Sonata*

Composer Aaron Copland

for *Three Unaccompanied Kettledrums* (1953), Alan Boustead's *Sonata for Timpani* (1960), and Alan Ridout's *Sonatina for Timpani* (1967). Elliot Carter has written several, including Six *Pieces for Kettledrums* (1960), and *Canto and Adagio* (1966). Reginald Smith Brindle, an eminent contemporary percussionist and author of books on percussion, has contributed *Concert Piece for Timpani* (1967).

There are more, but again, this is the time to refer to a genuine list of suggested listening — rather than a list disguised as a paragraph.

The century isn't over yet, and the creative storm shows no signs of dying out. Who knows? Perhaps you'll be a part of it.

Béla Bartók's Concerto for
Two Pianos, Percussion, and Orchestra
*is a challenging piece even
to the most skilled percussionists.*

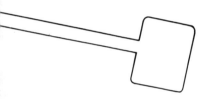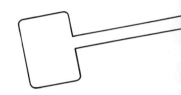

THE MODERN PERCUSSION SECTION

It's time to take a closer look at the standard array of instruments available to the percussionist in a modern symphony orchestra, and to see how these instruments have evolved to meet current demands.

Generally, the percussionist will have at his disposal three timpani whose heads measure twenty-four inches, twenty-six inches, and twenty-nine and a half inches across, covering a range of an octave and a third. A drum may be capable of producing several different tones (depending on the tension applied to the membrane), but its best tone is produced in the middle of its range. The percussionist is happiest when his drum supply is sufficient that no drum must be forced to the outer limits of its range, but the ideal arrangement of one tone per

A view of the New York Philharmonic.
Notice the xylophones, piano, and cymbals
as well as the array of different drums.

drum would pack the stage with sixteen drums in all. Consequently, convenience has triumphed over the ideal; pedal-tuned drums are now nearly universal, and the maximum number to be found onstage for a performance is usually five.

The bowl of the kettledrum is usually made of copper, although recent years have seen the introduction of the lighter and more durable fiber glass, which seems to produce a satisfactory tone as well. The head, once (and, occasionally, still) made of calfskin, is now usually made of plastic, for reasons of durability and resistance to climatic changes. The Dresden model kettledrum, a pedal-tuned drum with a *sawtooth clutch,* which is the part of the head-tightening mechanism that locks it in place, is the most widely used.

The orchestral bass drum, suspended in a steel frame, is now up to forty inches wide and twenty inches deep, with a wooden shell. Distin, the manufacturer who introduced the shallow side drum around 1850, once produced a "monster bass drum" with a membrane some eight feet across; the membrane was allegedly made from the hide of a buffalo. (The marching band with the University of Chicago football team used to play a drum of comparable size during half-time shows, but somebody stored it too close to a nuclear reactor under the stadium bleachers, with the result that it is now too radioactive to play.)

The tips, called *acorns,* on unpadded bass-drum beaters are made of either hardwood or hard felt. Soft felt or lamb's wool is used for the padded beaters.

The side drum has undergone many changes since its ancestors came to Europe with the Crusaders. The most substantial changes were the introduction of *rod-tensioning* — a system for changing the tension of drumheads through the use of rods and

A percussionist surrounded by his instruments:
kettledrums, snare (or side) drum,
xylophone, glockenspiel, and electric organ

a screw mechanism — and the shallow shell in the middle of the nineteenth century. Although side drums still come in a variety of sizes, the present standard is five to eight inches deep and fourteen or fifteen inches across the head.

The shell is made of wood or metal. The two heads, made of calfskin or plastic, are independently tensioned; the snare is on the lower (and thinner) head. The snare, which is vital to the sound, is made of nylon, wire, gut, or wire-covered silk. A wide variety of sticks is used, and although the layman might not be able to detect some of the subtle differences between them, the trained percussionist has no trouble at all.

As for the tenor drum, so popular with Stravinsky, Milhaud, Copland, Britten, Honegger, and others, it is generally wider than it is deep — approximately eighteen inches by fourteen inches. It has two heads, but no snare. The tone is somewhere between the tones of the side and bass drums.

The modern tabor is an instrument distinct from the side drum; it is deeper than it is wide and comes in several sizes. On the beaten head is a single snare made of gut, silk, or hemp. The head is usually made, again, of plastic, and wire snares are becoming more common. These concessions to progress are made in the name of durability, although whether or not the tone is improved could be debated.

Then of course there is the standard array of cymbals, triangle, woodblock, tam-tam, Turkish crescent, and on to the xylophone and glockenspiel (which can hardly be classified as drums).

In addition to kettledrums, modern percussion sections usually include the snare drum (or side drum)—above; the orchestral bass drum—left; and the tenor drum—right.

In addition, there may be any number of special contrivances, depending on the composition at hand. Chains are sometimes called for (as in Schoenberg's *Gurrelieder*). H. Davidson's *Auto Accident* demands that the percussionist break some glass and dump it onto a hard surface. William Russell's *Three Dance Movements* requires hammer, saw-blade (to be drawn across a cymbal), ginger ale bottle (to be smashed), and a wooden stick covered with rubber bands for use in striking cymbals.

It would seem that nearly everything that can be struck to produce a sound is now fair game in composing for percussion.

If, at this point, you think that every possible use to which percussion might be put has been explored, you are about to see that this is far from the case. There are two energetic, creative, and essentially American musical genres waiting to be examined in the next two chapters, and it is now time to see what they are all about.

JAZZ

Whereas the history of drums in their classical context is primarily the history of composers and equipment, the story of their roles in both jazz and rock — as is true of any folk art — is basically the story of the musicians who have played them.

The stature of jazz today is somewhat ironic in that, while it was once held to be a mainly black music, the illiterate product of uneducated (if gifted) people, it is now widely viewed as a rather esoteric and mysterious music, the exclusive domain of abstract and intellectual folks, black and white, who wander around in berets and sunglasses, grooving on intricate vibrations that are incomprehensible to the man on the street.

This is a rather intriguing turn of events, since

jazz got from where it began to where it is today by passing through a heavily commercial epoch during which it was the essential popular music of America.

But first: what is jazz? The people who love it would be hard-pressed to define it. It isn't really hopelessly esoteric, but it certainly is not illiterate either — as illustrated by the music of such masters as Don Ellis and the late Duke Ellington.

It might be defined, if rather drily, as a synthesis — a combination of musical elements from several different traditions. Rhythm is certainly an essential part of the definition, as illustrated by the fact that the most important jazz magazine in America is named *Downbeat*. Jazz seems to be the musical tradition that resulted from the fusion, early in this century, of primarily African concepts of rhythm and structure with the melodic and harmonic elements of European music — heavily influenced by the popularity during that era of marching bands and minstrel shows. Perhaps the most important factor is *improvisation*; jazz musicians create much of their music as it is being played; they are not just reading notes on a score.

A very limited definition, to be sure. Your true jazz aficionado begins to steam with indignation at the very suggestion that jazz can be defined at all. Jazz is as indefinable as the taste of an avocado. You don't define jazz — you listen to it.

It should be emphasized that there isn't even agreement as to what can be included in this indefinable music. There are traditionalists who maintain that jazz is an exclusively improvisational music, that the conscious application of training and music theory are corruptions — or at least changes — of an art that should be approached with a self-conscious sense of preservation — operating only within certain limits. Conversely, some modernists feel that any music composed or played by a person who is inspired by (and reverent toward) the tradition in general

The late Duke Ellington,
a master of jazz

is entitled to be called jazz — no matter how many semesters the composer may have spent studying at the Juilliard School. Like all debates in all areas of art, this one really hasn't a prayer of being resolved.

So we must be content with a broad examination of the music that has been called jazz by any number of people. Fortunately, there are lines of continuity that can be traced from the beginning of the century to the present, lines that can be used, perhaps, to hold our queasy definition of jazz together. That continuity takes the form of influence or inspiration. The person who learned to play the music that he or she plays by listening largely to music that was called jazz by the people who played it may be entitled to be called a jazz musician — and it is the history of such people that we should explore.

There is a widely accepted myth that jazz was born in New Orleans — germinated there, grew there, burst forth from there, and spread throughout the land. Like all myths, it is convenient; like all myths, it isn't quite true. To say that jazz was born in New Orleans is to say that the very similar social and creative energies that abounded in other areas of the country were somehow static, and that the musicians in these areas were passing the time with finger exercises while waiting to be overwhelmed by the good news from Louisiana.

No, the jazz genesis occurred simultaneously in several places at once — Chicago, Kansas City, Harlem, and St. Louis, to name a few. Cross-influences were certainly numerous and New Orleans definitely played a larger role than any other single place.

The very early jazz bands had two drummers, one on snare drum and the other on bass drum and cymbal. This was one noticeable influence of the marching bands. The role of the drummer in those days of jazz was very basic, for two reasons. For one thing, jazz musicians have always seen their music as a fusion of three elements: rhythm, melody, and harmony. A jazz drum solo was long felt (if unconsciously) to be a contradiction in terms; a drum solo was only one-third jazz.

Secondly, since much jazz certainly did come from poor, urban blacks, there wasn't a lot of money for equipment, and the dazzling array of instruments with which a modern drummer can now work out wasn't even a dream. The early jazz drummer generally had at his disposal one snare drum, two or three small Chinese tom-toms, and a cymbal or two — usually no bass drum. In those days the drummer was little more than a timekeeper. Only occasionally did drummers get individual attention — when they functioned as clowns, providing the comedy.

There were some good drummers keeping good time even in those days, though, and there were men who would be heard from later when the role of the drum expanded.

In New Orleans, Zutty Singleton was getting his first exposure around 1920. He would prove to be one of the eminent drummers of the swing era, when the big bands came on the scene in the early 1920s. Jack "Papa" Laine was another major figure in early New Orleans. Considered to be one of the founders of jazz, he led many superb groups, such as the Reliance Brass Band, and gave support to men who would make names for themselves later on — Tom Brown, trombonist George Brunies, and many others. In New York, Arthur "Traps" McIntyre and Tony Sbarboro (better known as Tony Spargo) were making themselves known during the first World War.

Three important developments occurred shortly before 1920. Warren "Baby" Dodds, another important figure in early New Orleans, began using a foot-pedal bass drum, a move that was eventually to be universally imitated. In addition, the Turkish cymbal manufacturer A. Zildjian introduced a line of cymbals that were far superior to anything previously used. (Zildjian's American affiliate, K. Zildjian, now manufactures cymbals in the United States as well.) Finally, Vic Berton began using foot-cymbals in the early twenties; he was one of the first to use the pedal-operated "high-hat" cymbal, and he even used timpani on occasion — tuned in octaves. Though these changes increased the number of things a drummer could do, drums remained mainly in the background.

Warren "Baby" Dodds was
born in New Orleans in 1848.

Then came the revolutionary development of recorded sound, which transformed jazz as it did every other kind of music, bringing wide recognition to some other drummers who were destined to become legends.

Ben Pollack, who played with the New Orleans Rhythm Kings (notice the name of the group), was the first white drummer to achieve any success in the jazz world. The significance of his achievement is substantial; before that time, many people (both inside the jazz world and out) believed that only black musicians could develop an authentic feel for jazz. After Pollack it was recognized (more rapidly in some circles than in others) that no one group of people could lay exclusive claim to any style of music. Granted that the jazz played by white musicians was often more commercial, the heritage of jazz music as it exists today has drawn heavily on the influences of a multitude of talented people.

Pollack went on to organize his own band in the mid-1930s. He was replaced in the Rhythm Kings by Ray Bauduc, another important figure in Dixieland jazz.

The South Side of Chicago was the scene of a great deal of jazz activity during the late 1920s and early 1930s, and it was unusual in that it was racially integrated. From Zutty Singleton, Baby Dodds, and others, a small group of white musicians was learning the tricks of the trade first-hand.

Dave Tough, a tireless man, was there developing the style that would take him from small combos to prominence with the big bands of Tommy Dorsey, Woody Herman, and Benny Goodman. George Wettling, who would be associated with the modernized, Dixieland style that would be known as "Nicksieland" (after Nick's, the Greenwich Village club in New York City where much of it originated) was there, plying the pros for information.

And there was Gene Krupa.

People who know almost nothing about jazz have heard of Krupa. It was during his internship in Chicago that he developed, through constant experimentation and inexhaustible curiosity, the style that would make him a legend. It was Krupa who, with McKenzie and Condon's Chicagoans in 1928, made the first known recording on which a bass drum was used.

In the late thirties, as star drummer with Benny Goodman, the gum-chewing Krupa became an idol to millions; it was his solo performance on *Sing, Sing, Sing,* on record and at the Carnegie Hall jazz concert in 1937, that showed the world how a drum could be used as a solo instrument. It was a major turning point in the history of jazz drumming.

The years between 1937 and 1942 were a time of prominence for Jonathan "Jo" Jones, who would serve as an inspiration to Kenny Clarke, Max Roach, and Art Blakey. He had a singular high-hat technique, and was one of the first to syncopate the rhythms played on the bass drum.

Cozy Cole, who collaborated with Krupa during the 1950s in the operation of a drum school, was every bit as flamboyant, although he believed that the drummer's job was to provide the strongest rhythmic background, not to dominate the music. But the versatility and functional beat that he provided for the swing bands of Cab Calloway, Stuff Smith, Willie Bryant, and Louis Armstrong established him as one of the all-time greats.

During the thirties, jazz was king — but in a form that would scarcely be recognized by the jazzmakers of twenty years earlier. Large and boisterous orchestras played carefully arranged compositions with tight harmonies; these were the big bands of the swing era, and they reigned supreme during the two decades of the big-band craze. They were showcases for talent; an exceptional performer might be with a band only briefly before winning widespread renown and going to form a band of his own. The bands of Benny Goodman, Woody Herman, Harry James, Louis Armstrong, Tommy Dorsey, Cab Calloway, Count Basie,

*Cozy Cole and Gene Krupa in
a scene from the movie,
The Glenn Miller Story, in 1953.*

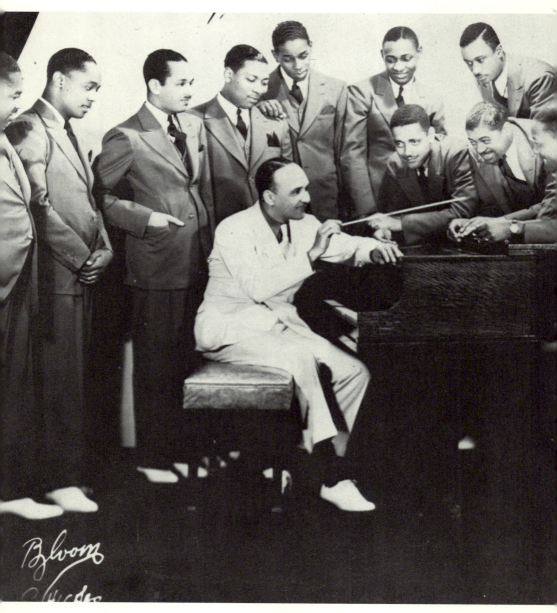

*The Fletcher Henderson Orchestra
in the late 1920s.*

Fletcher Henderson, Duke Ellington, Stan Kenton, and Artie Shaw gave more music to the world than had any other genre in a similar period of time.

Another man who set examples that other drummers followed was Chick Webb. Webb, who led his own group during the thirties, was Gene Krupa's idol: an eclectic, masterfully controlled drummer whose energy was all the more remarkable due to poor health during the last years of his life.

Modern drumming really began with Krupa, Webb, and Jo Jones, whose ability to function as soloists was responsible for a profound change in attitude toward the drummer's role in a jazz band.

But there were also those like Big Sid Catlett. One of the steadiest and most versatile drummers of the day, he played with the bands of Benny Carter, Fletcher Henderson, and Louis Armstrong. In addition he contributed to numerous recordings — such as the early bop era records of Dizzy Gillespie and Charlie Parker — that have since become classics. Like Cozy Cole, Catlett felt that a drummer should strive to shade and underline the music that was being defined by the rest of the band.

In contrast, again, stands Lionel Hampton, who has never had any reservations about making himself highly visible. From his early days with Louis Armstrong through his stint with Benny Goodman (who expanded his trio to a quartet to accommodate Hampton) to the formation of his own band in 1940, Hampton has always been a showman, as well as a master of the entire percussion spectrum — particularly vibraphone. There have been occasional complaints that his musicianship suffers as a consequence, but they never slow Hampton down.

The style of music that led to the stereotyped image of the jazz aficionado as an attic-dwelling, finger-snapping beatnik had its beginnings in the early 1940s with the music of Kenny Clarke. As early as 1940, Clarke's disaffection with the beat-pounding monotony of the bass drum prompted him to move the main beat from the bass drum to the top cymbal. He was the driving force behind the formation of many early bop bands, and his influence was strongly felt by Max Roach, Roy Haines, Shelly Manne, and Art Blakey. His fondness for more intimate sounds than those produced by the big bands marks him as the father of postswing drumming; what he didn't do himself was done by those he inspired, notably Max Roach.

Roach is always a performer, a joy to watch; he began recording with Dizzy Gillespie and Charlie Parker in the mid-forties, and soon had his own band. Roach was probably the first drummer to emphasize the melodic element in drumming, to see music in the drum as well as rhythm. More than any other performer of the time, he showed that the modern jazz drum could be as complex and expressive as any other instrument.

Dave Tough, who established himself through performances with Dorsey, Goodman, and Herman, was an extraordinary performer, unfazed by any change of style. He was thus equipped to survive the twilight of big-band jazz, a twilight that saw the prominence of some of swing's most talented men: Stan Levey; Art Blakey; Shelly Manne (who went on to form his own group, probably best known by national audiences as the house band at Mother's Bar in the television series, "Peter Gunn"); Buddy Rich (a child vaudeville drum act who came to jazz in the late thirties and a showman on a par with Roach); and Louis Bellson, who wasn't content with one bass drum — he uses two.

Then there are those fleeting, shadowy will-o'-the-wisps who show great promise and then fade from view or die young, becoming legends: men like Ike Day, Shadow Wilson, Frank Butler, Art Mardigan, Frank Isola, Lou Fromm, and Laurence Marable.

Between 1948 and 1954, Norman "Tiny" Kahn had a brief but distinguished career. As short as that career was, he remains widely admired and imitated.

The take-over of rock and roll in the 1950s left many of the superb jazz musicians somewhat cynical about finance and commerce, and they began to concentrate on a music that would fit into small clubs — a fact that perhaps contributed to the creation

At the Paris Jazz Festival in 1949,
drummer Kenny Clarke (left) poses with two
female jazz singers and another jazz musician.

of an attic/basement/beatnik mystique. The transformed jazz continued to be excellent music, but it became less demonstrative and more exploratory. The flexible structure and improvisation to which small clubs were conducive polarized the jazz audience: the big-band fans, who were left with their memories and a few surviving bands of nostalgic sounds; and the progressives, who grabbed their bongos and moved downstairs.

But the music went on. Manne, Blakey, Rich, Roach, Bellson, Levey, and such new talents as Joe Morello and "Philly Joe" Jones survived the transition and embraced the exploratory nature of their situation. These musicians found themselves with a new generation of admirers whose freedom from nostalgia made them receptive to whatever new and unusual experiments were being conducted.

In the now separate, experimental world of modern jazz, whose devotees are actually as numerous and loyal as they were twenty years ago, the influence of Roach, Blakey, and Clarke continues. Such highly professional "studio men" — in the old sense of the term meaning trained musicians who can play from a chart on sight — as Ed Shaughnessy, Grady Tate, Frank Capp, Sol Gubin, and Jack Sperling are consistently excellent and versatile. In jazz today, though, there seem to be very few showmen in the Krupa tradition; the role of the drummer these days again seems to be to lend his authority to lines established by the other musicians in his group. That authority is intact, however, and the listening list at the end of this book should give you some idea about where to look for it.

As the sixties and then the seventies unfolded, jazz continued to attract new faces. People like Elvin Jones, Tony Williams, Billy Cobham, and others promise that there is still life to spare in the genre.

Buddy Rich

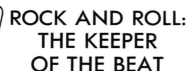

ROCK AND ROLL:
THE KEEPER
OF THE BEAT

In the early 1950s at the end of the big-band era, we are obviously confronted with the question of why that era ended. It is an easier question to answer than any question concerning its origins. It is a question with two answers: electronics and the birth of rock and roll.

Perhaps it seems remarkable now that nobody saw rock coming, but apparently nobody did. Only after it had taken the music world by storm, transforming the economics of the industry and undermining the financial base of the big bands in the process, did anybody fully appreciate that a profound and irreversible change had occurred.

Early rock drumming is easy to write (and read) about because the role of the drummer was set back about forty-five years. Despite their access to everything with which jazz drummers were so bewilderingly experimenting, rock drummers found themselves reduced to timekeeper status, their function being to provide four obvious beats per measure. The most devoted early rock and roll fan would probably be at a loss if asked for the name of the drummer on *Teen Angel*. The most exhaustive book on rock won't tell you who he was. Style was incidental, and so, therefore, were the identities of any would-be stylists.

Not that drums weren't important. On the contrary, drums may have been more important to the overall effect of early rock than they were to any previous music. The importance of "the Beat" in rock is axiomatic. But if rhythm is the heartbeat of rock, the essence of that rhythm in the early days demanded no more of the listener's attention than the beating of your heart does of yours. Drums were both central and peripheral, an interesting paradox.

Ask any rock fan to identify an important early rock drummer, and chances are that the name most likely to come up will be Sandy Nelson, who enjoyed some top-forty success in 1961 with two hit records — drum solos, 45-RPM curiosities.

It wasn't until the Beatles revolutionized rock the way rock had revolutionized music in general that drummers developed significance as individuals. The first celebrity drummer of the age was, of course, Ringo Starr. There are those who will be amused by the suggestion that Starr's fame is deserved, rather than just a by-product of the legitimate fame awarded to the other three Beatles. While it is true that Starr is a role-player, and not on a level with Krupa, he has one of the finest senses of rhythm in the business. His control is excellent and his shadings consistently appropriate.

Beatlemania, and the composer-performers that followed (a trend that was new to popular music, though certainly not to jazz), gave the world a number of celebrity drummers, whose emphasis was much more frequently on technical proficiency

Rock drummer, Ginger Baker.

The Beatles. The first celebrity drummer
of the new rock age was Ringo Starr.

than was the emphasis of the previous decade. Two of the first big names to come out of rock were Charlie Watts, of the Rolling Stones, and Billy Mundi, who first earned his stripes with Frank Zappa's Mothers of Invention by proving himself equal to the demands of Zappa's involved compositions. There is Nigel Olsen, who is never at a loss in providing appropriate backing for Elton John. Rock music has also given the world Dino Danelli of the Rascals; Mitch Mitchell, who played drums for Jimi Hendrix; Bobby Colomby of Blood, Sweat, and Tears; and Danny Seraphine of Chicago (the group as well as the city).

Hal Blaine, a truly professional and consistent musician, is probably one of the leading studio drummers in America (he's the one on all those Simon and Garfunkel albums); with Russ Kunkel, whose stamp is on countless hours of recorded music by many groups and soloists, running a close second.

And of course there is Ginger Baker, formerly of Cream, whose blistering, twenty-minute drum solo, *Toad*, is already a rock classic. Baker is also responsible for another rare touch: his use of kettledrums, tuned to four distinct pitches, for Cream's recording of *White Room*.

Drums obviously have no intention of going away; it's hard to imagine what the music of the past two centuries would have been like without them. It is ridiculous to try, actually, since the love of rhythm that leads to musical creativity assures us that rhythm instruments will continue to be a part of it.

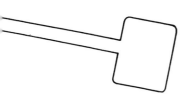

MEET
THE
MAKERS

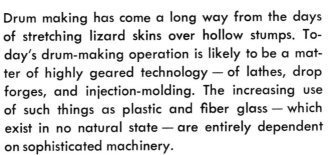

Drum making has come a long way from the days of stretching lizard skins over hollow stumps. Today's drum-making operation is likely to be a matter of highly geared technology — of lathes, drop forges, and injection-molding. The increasing use of such things as plastic and fiber glass — which exist in no natural state — are entirely dependent on sophisticated machinery.

Although there is much to be said for the precision that a vellum of precisely calculated thickness gives — a thickness that is uniform throughout — some traditionalists decry the trend away from the authenticity of calfskin. There is no conclusive evidence that plastic heads improve the tone of a drum. But the advantage of a drumhead that doesn't get damp and cranky whenever the humidity changes is obvious, as is the reduced tendency of plastic drumheads to break in the middle of a performance. Plastic and fiber glass are easier materials to work with, and less expensive as well.

The most widely accepted kettledrum these days is the Dresden model, a pedal-operated drum with a sawtooth clutch that locks the mechanism in place and prevents it from slipping.

Leaders among the drum-making nations are Germany, Britain, and the United States. The Germans have a long tradition of progress and quality in the making of drums, and the best ones there are made by Ringer Apparatebau of Berlin, and Spenke & Metzl, Dresdner Apparatebau in Dresden. Germany is more inclined to use traditional materials, using more copper, wood, and calfskin than other countries.

The best English drums are made by the Premier Drum Company, James and William Bradshaw, L. W. Hunt, Ringer, Boosey & Hawkes, and Kurt Goedicke.

The United States, by virtue of sheer size, probably has more drummers than any other nation in the Western Hemisphere, a fact that is reflected in the number of drums made here. The Ludwig Drum Company, one of the oldest and largest American firms, is familiar to just about everyone who ever played drums in a high school marching or dance band. America is also the home of the Slingerland Drum Company, the Leedy Drum Company, the Rogers Drum Company, and many more.

There aren't too many people left who make drums on anything resembling an individual basis. One who does is Walter J. Light, percussionist with the Denver Symphony Orchestra. His American Dresden Pedal Timpani, made on a production scale that is quite small by industry standards, are regarded as among the finest.

Drum bowls and frames,
manufactured at Ludwig
Industries in Chicago

Whether or not the world gets terribly excited about drum makers, they are among the most fundamentally important men in music. It is their technology and standards that allow composers to extract from percussion instruments the wide range of effects, both subtle and dazzling, without which music would be a far less effective art form.

Saul Goodman, percussionist
with the New York Philharmonic,
working in his timpani shop

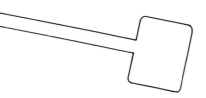

WHITHER THE BEAT?

There are several possible explanations for why you picked up this book in the first place. Perhaps you were just curious. Perhaps the thought of being a drummer appealed to you, but you were not sure it was challenging enough to get serious about.

Perhaps it was assigned reading.

Whatever your reasons, this book was not so much an attempt to tell you everything there is to know about drums as it was an attempt to suggest that there is indeed a great deal that can be known, and that the opportunities for exploring the world of percussion can prove themselves a worthy challenge to your energies. Hopefully, you have gained a greater understanding of the importance of percussion, of its colorful history, and of the many forms it takes in the world of music today.

If you choose to become a drummer, you will be becoming, in a sense, indispensable. Take one violinist out of a fifty-member string section, and the show will go on with little apparent change. But remove the percussionist, and things become hopelessly crippled. The great composers of the past two centuries have understood this, and their consequent respect for percussion is reflected in their work.

From Babylonia to Bartók to Brubeck, the drum has been with us since feet began to tap. And as long as there are feet, they'll be tapping, and they'll need somebody to help them keep time.

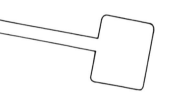

SUGGESTED LISTENING

THE CLASSICAL TRADITION

Bartók, Béla

   Concerto for Two Pianos, Percussion, and Orchestra. Bernstein, New York Philharmonic Orchestra. Columbia MS-6956.

   Sonata for Two Pianos and Percussion. Ponse, Dorati, et al. London Symphony Orchestra. Mercury 90515.

Bax, Arnold

   Tintagel. Barbirolli, London Symphony Orchestra. Angel S-36415.

Beethoven, Ludwig van

   Missa Solemnis in D, Op. 123. Farrell, Bernstein, et al. New York Philharmonic Orchestra. Columbia M2S-619.

   Symphony No. 9 in D, Op. 125. Solti, Chicago Symphony Orchestra and Chorus. London CSP-8.

Berlioz, Hector

   Beatrice et Benedict. Veasey, Davis, et al. London Symphony Orchestra. Oiseau S-256/7.

The Music of Berlioz. Bernstein, Ormandy, et al. Columbia M-30384.

Symphonie Fantastique, Op. 14. Klemperer, Philadelphia Orchestra. Angel S-36196.

Britten, Benjamin

Young Person's Guide to the Orchestra, Op. 34. Bernstein, New York Philharmonic Orchestra. Columbia S-31808.

Cage, John

Amores for Prepared Piano and Percussion. Manhattan Percussion Ensemble. Mainstream 5011.

Copland, Aaron

Concerto for Piano and Orchestra. Copland, Bernstein, New York Philharmonic Orchestra. Columbia MS-6698.

Music for a Great City. Copland, London Symphony Orchestra. Columbia M-30374.

Statements for Orchestra. Copland, London Symphony Orchestra. Everest 3015.

Debussy, Claude

La Mer. Szell, Cleveland Orchestra. Odyssey Y-31928.

The Music of Debussy. Ormandy, Bernstein, et al. Columbia MS-7523.

Haydn, Franz Joseph

The Creation. Ameling, Spoorenberg, et al. Vienna Philharmonic Orchestra and State Opera Chorus. London 1271.

Hindemith, Paul

Kammermusik No. 5, Op. 36/4; No. 6, Op. 46/1. Doktor, Vermeulen, Concerto Amsterdam. Telefunken 22527.

Holst, Gustav

The Planets, Op. 32. Herrmann, London Philharmonic Orchestra. London 21049.

Honegger, Arthur

Pacific 231. Ansermet, Orchestre Suisse Romande. London 6367.

Janácek, Leos

Jenufa. Prague National Theatre. Angel S-3756.

Sinfonietta. Szell, Cleveland Symphony Orchestra. Columbia MS-6815.

Lully, Jean Baptiste

Thesée (selections). Mattei, Ayer, et al. Vienna Volksoper Orchestra. RCA VICS-1686.

Mahler, Gustav

Symphony No. 1 in D. Solti, London Symphony Orchestra. London 6401.

Milhaud, Darius

Concerto for Percussion and Small Orchestra. Daniel, Milhaud, Luxemburg Radio Orchestra. Candide 31013.

Nielsen, Carl

Symphony No. 4 (Inextinguishable). Bernstein, New York Philharmonic Orchestra. Columbia M-30293.

Symphony No. 5, Op. 50. Bernstein, New York Philharmonic Orchestra. Columbia MS-6414.

Poulenc, Francis

Concerto in G for Organ, Strings, and Timpani. Biggs, Ormandy, Philadelphia Orchestra. Columbia MS-6398.

Prokofiev, Serge

Symphony in D. Bernstein, New York Philharmonic Orchestra. Columbia MS-7528.

Purcell, Henry

The Fairy Queen. Vyvyan, Britten, et al. English Chamber Orchestra. London 1290.

Ode for St. Cecilia's Day. Tiffin Chorus, Ambrosian Singers, English Chamber Orchestra. Deutsche Grammophon Archive 2533042.

Ravel, Maurice

Bolero. Ormandy, Philadelphia Orchestra. Columbia MS-7673.

Saint-Saëns, Camille

Samson et Delila. Vickers, Gorr, et al. Angel S-3639.

Satie, Erik

Trois Gymnopédies. Previn, London Symphony Orchestra. RCA LSC-2945.

Schoenberg, Arnold

Five Pieces for Orchestra. Craft, Cleveland Symphony Orchestra. Columbia M2S-709.

Gurrelieder. Borkh, Topper, et al. Bavarian Radio Orchestra and Chorus. Deutsche Grammophon 2707022.

Stravinsky, Igor

The Firebird. Stravinsky, Columbia Symphony Orchestra. Columbia D3S-705.

L'Histoire du Soldat: Suite. Stravinsky, Columbia Symphony Orchestra. Columbia MS-6272.

Petrouchka. Stravinsky, Columbia Symphony Orchestra. Columbia MS-6332.

Le Sacre du Printemps. Stravinsky, Columbia Symphony Orchestra. Columbia MS-6272.

Strauss, Richard

Elektra, Op. 58. Nilsson, Collier, et al. Vienna Philharmonic Orchestra. London 1269.

Rosenkavalier. Ormandy, Philadelphia Orchestra. Columbia MS-6678.

Salome. Nilsson, Stolze, et al. Vienna Philharmonic Orchestra. London 1218.

Till Eulenspiegel, Op. 28. Bernstein, New York Philharmonic Orchestra. Columbia MS-6225.

Varèse, Edgard

Hyperprism. Cerha, "Die Reihe" Ensemble. Candide 31028.

Ionisation. Mehta, Los Angeles Philharmonic. London 6752.

Webern, Anton

Im Sommerwind; 3 Pieces for Orchestra. Ormandy, Philadelphia Orchestra. Columbia MS-7041.

Weinberger, Jaromir

Schwanda: Polka and Fugue. Reiner, Chicago Symphony Orchestra. RCA VICS-1424.

JAZZ

African Drums. Folkways FE 4502.

Armstrong, Louis

Louis Armstrong. Audio Fidelity 6241.

The Louis Armstrong Story. Columbia ML 4383/4/5/6.

Louis "Satchmo" Armstrong. Archives of Folk & Jazz Music 258.

With the Dukes of Dixieland. Audio Fidelity 5924.

Basie, Count

Count Basie. MGM GAS-126.

Verve's Choice Best. Verve 68596.

Bechet, Sidney

Sidney Bechet Jazz Classics. Blue Note 1201.

Bellson, Louis

Big Bands! Onyx 202.

Blakey, Art

Big Beat. Blue Note 84029.

Holiday for Skins. Blue Note 84004/5.

Orgy in Rhythm. Blue Note 81554/5.

Night at Birdland. Blue Note 81521/2.

Brown, Clifford

Clifford Brown & Max Roach at Basin Street. Em Arcy 36070.

Brubeck, Dave

At Carnegie Hall. Columbia C2S-826.

Brubeck on Campus. Columbia KG-31298.

Brubeck Plays Bernstein, Bernstein Plays Brubeck. Columbia CS-8257.

Gone with the Wind. Columbia CS-8156.
Newport 1958. Columbia CSP JCS-8082.
Clarke, Kenny
  Paris Bebop Sessions. Prestige S-7605.
Coltrane, John
  The Greatest Years. Impulse S-9200.
  "Live" at the Village Vanguard. Impulse S-10.
  Soultrane. Prestige S-7531.
Ellington, Duke
  The Best of Duke Ellington. Capitol DT-1602.
  Ellington Indigos. Columbia CS-8053.
  The First Time (with Count Basie). Columbia CS-8515.
  Money Jungle (with Mingus & Roach). United Artists 5632.
Ellis, Don
  Electric Bath. Columbia CS-9585.
  "Live" at Monterey. Pacific Jazz 20112.
  Soaring. BASF 25123.
Getz, Stan
  The Stan Getz Quartet at Storyville. Roost 2209.
Gillespie, Dizzy
  Dizzier and Dizzier. RCA LJM-1009.
Giuffre, Jimmy
  Tangents in Jazz. Capitol T634.
Goodman, Benny
  Benny Goodman Combos. Columbia GL 500.
Hamilton, Chico
  The Best of Chico Hamilton. Impulse S-9174.
  The Chico Hamilton Quintet. Pacific Jazz PJ-1225.
  Exigente. Flying Dutchman 10135.
  His Great Hits. Impulse 9213.
Hampton, Lionel
  Hot Mallets. RCA LJM 1000.
Henderson, Fletcher
  The Birth of Big Band Jazz. Riverside RLP 12-129.
Herman, Woody
  Concerto for Herd. Verve 68764.
  Heavy Exposure. Cadet S-835.
  The Three Herds. Columbia CL 592.
  Woody. Cadet 845.
Holiday, Billie
  Billie Holiday. Commodore FL-30008.

The Jazz Messengers (Art Blakey)
The Jazz Messengers at the Cafe Bohemia. Blue Note 1507.
Jones, Thad
Jazz Collaborations (with Charlie Mingus). Debut 17.
Kenton, Stan
Deluxe Set. Capitol STCL-2989.
Stan Kenton. Capitol STCL-575.
Today. London 44179/80.
Konitz, Lee
Lee Konitz (with Warne Marsh). Atlantic 1217.
Krupa, Gene
Gene Krupa and His Orchestra. Columbia CL 6017.
Let Me Off Uptown. Verve 68571.
Percussion King. Verve 68414.
Verve's Choice Best. Verve 68594.
Mann, Herbie
The Best of Herbie Mann. Prestige S-7432.
Big Boss. Columbia CS-1068.
Family of Mann. Atlantic S-1371.
Manne, Shelly
Alive in London. Contemporary 7629.
At the Mannehole. Contemporary 7593/4.
My Son, the Drummer. Contemporary 7609.
Peter Gunn. Contemporary 7560.
The Modern Jazz Quartet
Best of the Modern Jazz Quartet. Atlantic S-1546.
Classics. Prestige S-7425.
First Recordings! Prestige S-7749.
The Modern Jazz Quartet. Prestige 160.
Space. Apple STAO-3360.
The Original Blues Project
Reunion in Central Park. MCA 2-8003.
Parker, Charlie
All-Star Sextet (with Max Roach). Roost 2210.
Bird and Diz (with Dizzy Gillespie). Verve 68006.
Charlie Parker. Prestige 24009.
The Charlie Parker Story. Verve 68000/1/2.
The Essential Charlie Parker (with Rich, Roach, Clarke). Verve V-8409.
Jazz Perennial. Verve 68009.
Peterson, Oscar
Oscar Peterson Plays Count Basie. Clef MG C 708.

Pollack, Ben
   Ben Pollack with Wingy Manone. Savoy 12207.
Rich, Buddy
   The Best of Buddy Rich. Pacific Jazz 20169.
   Buddy Rich. Archives of Folk & Jazz Music 260.
   Different Drummer. RCA LSP-4593.
   Rich vs. Roach (with Max Roach). Mercury 60133.
Roach, Max
   Drums Unlimited. Atlantic S-1467.
   It's Time. Impulse S-16.
   Percussion Bitter Sweet. Impulse S-8.
   Speak, Brother, Speak. Fantasy 86007.
Smith, Stuff
   Memorial Album. Prestige S-7691.
   W. Grappelly. Archives of Folk & Jazz Music 238.
Three Decades of Music
   1939-49, Volume 1. Blue Note 89902.
   1949-59, Volume 1. Blue Note 89903.
   1959-69, Volume 1. Blue Note 89904.
Webb, Chick
   On the Air. Trip J-5.
Young, Lester
   The Essential Lester Young (with Jo Jones). Verve V-8398.

ROCK

Band, The
   Cahoots. Capitol SMAS-651.
   Music from Big Pink. Capitol SKAO-2955.
Beatles, The
   Abbey Road. Apple SSO-383.
   The Beatles. Apple SWBO-101.
   Sergeant Pepper's Lonely Hearts Club Band. Capitol SMAS-2653.
Berry, Chuck
   The Golden Decade. Columbia CSS S-1514.
Blood, Sweat, and Tears
   Blood, Sweat, and Tears. Columbia SCS-9720.
   Child Is Father to the Man. Columbia SCS 9619.
   Volume 3. Columbia SKC-30090.
Booker T and the MG's
   Set. Stax 2009.

Up Tight. Stax 2006.

Chicago
 At Carnegie Hall, Vols. 1-4. 4-Columbia C4X-30865.
 Chicago. Columbia KC-32400.

Cream
 Disraeli Gears. Atco SD33-206.
 Fresh Cream. Atco SD33-232.
 Wheels of Fire, Atco SD2-700.

Haley, Bill, and His Comets
 Greatest Hits. Decca S-75027.

Jimi Hendrix Experience, The
 In the West. Reprise S-2049.
 Rare Hendrix. Trip 9500.
 Roots of Hendrix. Trip 9501.
 War Heroes. Reprise 2103.

Jefferson Airplane
 Long John Silver. Grunt FTR-1007.
 Surrealistic Pillow. RCA LSP-3766.

Mothers of Invention, The
 Absolutely Free. Verve SG-5013.
 Cruisin' with Reuben and the Jets. Verve VG-5055X.
 Freak Out. Verve VG-5005-2X.
 We're Only In It for the Money. Verve SG-5045.

Nelson, Sandy
 Let There Be Drums. Imperial S-12080.
 Manhattan Spiritual. Imperial S-12439.

Rascals, The
 Island of Real. Columbia KC-31103.
 Peaceful World. 2-Columbia G-30462.

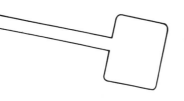

SUGGESTED
READING

Barzun, Jacques. *Berlioz and the Romantic Imagination.* Boston: Boston Book & Art Shop, 1969.

Belz, Carl. *The Story of Rock.* New York: Oxford University Press, 1969.

Berlioz, Hector, and Richard Wagner. *On Beethoven.* New York: Dover, 1970.

Blades, James. *Percussion Instruments and Their History.* New York: Praeger, 1970.

Bockman, Charles. *Cool, Hot, and Blue: A History of Jazz for Young People.* New York: Washington Square Press, 1970.

Boretz, Benjamin, and Edward Cone, eds. *Perspectives on Schoenberg and Stravinsky.* Princeton, N.J.: Princeton University Press.

Brindle, Reginald Smith. *Contemporary Percussion.* Fair Lawn, N.J.: Oxford University Press, 1970.

Charters, Samuel B. *Jazz: New Orleans, Eighteen Eighty-Five to Nineteen Sixty-Three.* (rev. ed.) New York: Oak Publications.

Condon, Eddie. *We Called It Music: A Generation of Jazz.* Westport, Conn.: Greenwood Press, 1947.

Copland, Aaron. *Copland on Music.* New York: W. W. Norton, 1963.

Dankworth, Avril. *Jazz: An Introduction to Its Musical Basis.* Fair Lawn, N.J.: Oxford University Press, 1968.

Dawson, Alan, and Don DeMichael. *Manual for the Modern Drummer.* Boston: Berklee Press.

Dobrin, Arnold. *Igor Stravinsky: His Life and Times.* New York: Thomas Y. Crowell, 1969.

Feather, Leonard. *The Book of Jazz: From Then Till Now.* New York: Horizon Press.

———. *The Encyclopedia of Jazz.* New York: Horizon Press.

Hentoff, Nat. *Journey into Jazz.* New York: Coward McCann, 1968.

Holst, Imogen. *Britten.* New York: Thomas Y. Crowell, 1966.

Howard, Joseph N. *Drums of the Americas.* New York: Oak Publications, 1966.

Jones, LeRoi. *Black Music.* New York: Apollo Editions, 1968.

Kettlekamp, Larry. *Drums, Rattles, and Bells.* New York: William Morrow, 1960.

Schuller, Gunther. *Early Jazz: Its Roots and Musical Development.* New York: Oxford University Press, 1968.

Shapiro, Nat, and Nat Hentoff, eds. *Hear Me Talkin' to Ya: The Story of Jazz by the Men Who Made It.* New York: Dover, 1966.

Shivas, A. A. *Art of the Timpanist and Drummer.* Chester Springs, Pa.: Dufour Editions, 1957.

Stevens, Halsey. *The Life and Music of Béla Bartók.* New York: Oxford University Press, 1967.

Stravinsky, Igor. *The Autobiography of Igor Stravinsky.* New York: W. W. Norton, 1962.

Taylor, Henry. *The Art and Science of the Timpani.* New York: Fernhill House, 1964.

Terkel, Studs. *Giants of Jazz.* New York: Thomas Y. Crowell, 1957.

Weil, Lisl. *Things That Go Bang.* New York: McGraw-Hill, 1969.

White, Eric. *W. Stravinsky: The Composer and His Works.* Berkeley, Calif.: University of California Press, 1969.

Williams, Martin. *Where's the Melody: A Listener's Introduction to Jazz.* New York: Minerva Press, Funk & Wagnalls, 1967.

Wilson, John S. *Jazz: The Transition Years, 1940–1960*. New York: Appleton Century, 1966.

Woerner, Karl H. *Schoenberg's Moses and Aaron*. New York: St. Martin's Press, 1959.

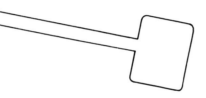 # GLOSSARY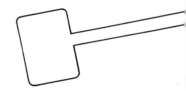

Atambor. Spanish for *tabor.*

Acorn. The small knob on the tip of an unpadded drumstick.

Acoustics. The science of sound, the study of its nature and behavior.

Chromatic scale. A scale that progresses in evenly spaced halftones — twelve tones in all to an octave.

Dissonance. A combination of tones not regarded in the usual sense as harmonious.

High-hat cymbal. A pair of opposed cymbals usually on a tripod stand, tapped together by means of a foot-pedal. Used mostly in jazz and rock music.

Idiophone. A percussion instrument made of a naturally sonorous material, such as the cymbal, woodblock, or triangle.

Improvisation. Spontaneous composition, the art of composing music while it is being played. Improvisation is characteristic of jazz.

Ingqongqo. A Bantu "drum" consisting of an animal hide stretched between four poles and beaten with sticks.

Interval. The difference in pitch between two notes or tones, played either simultaneously or consecutively.

Jannisary music. The martial (military). music of the Turkish army, a form of which was the nucleus of a musical fad in Europe during the middle 1700s.

Membranophone. A percussion instrument that produces sound by means of the vibration of a thin membrane, stretched tightly over a bowl, shell, or frame.

Nakers. A pair of Turkish military drums, on each of which a single membrane is stretched over a closed bowl. Introduced into Europe during the twelfth century, it was the precursor of the modern pair of timpani.

Rod-tensioning. A system for loosening or tightening drumheads (used on bass drums, snare drums, and tenor drums) involving threaded rods and a screw mechanism. First introduced by the manufacturer Distin around 1850.

Sawtooth clutch. On a kettledrum, the part of the head-tightening mechanism that locks it into place; the teeth keep the mechanism from slipping.

Screw-tensioning. A system of tightening or loosening the head of a kettledrum involving hand-turned screws.

Serial music. A system of composition devised by Arnold Schoenberg. Serial music involves a "tone row," rather than a melody in the traditional sense, in which all twelve tones of the chromatic scale must be played before any tone can be repeated. The sequence of tones is fixed at the discretion of the composer, although a tone can be placed in any octave or given any emphasis (quarter-note, half-note, etc.).

Snare. A strand of wire, gut, wire-covered silk, or nylon that rests against one head of a drum for the purpose of producing a briefly sustained rattling or "sizzling" sound when the head is struck.

Sympathetic vibration. The vibration of an object in response to vibrations transmitted through the air from another object that is already vibrating.

Syncopation. Shifting of the musical emphasis by placing the accent on a normally nonaccented beat.

Taberett. Old English word for the *tabor.*

Tabor. A small drum introduced into Europe by either the Crusaders or the Moors during the twelfth century. It had a snare and two membranes of sheepskin or calfskin. Beaten with a single stick or beater, it was about a foot in diameter and two feet deep. The modern tabor is generally smaller (still deeper than it is wide), having membranes that are usually made of plastic, with a snare on the beaten head.

Taboret. French word for the early *tabor.*

Tambourin. German and French word for the early *tabor.*

Tamburino. Italian word for the early *tabor.*

Tam-tam. A medium-sized gong with indefinite pitch.

Timpani. A pair or set of kettledrums, especially as used in a band or orchestra.

Tonality. The melodic or harmonic relationships between the tones of a musical system or scale.

Turkish crescent. A long pole with a metallic, crescent-shaped head from which small bells are hung to produce an indefinitely pitched jingling sound.

Vellum. Drumhead or membrane.

INDEX

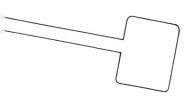 

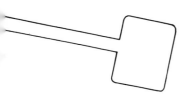

ABOUT THE AUTHOR

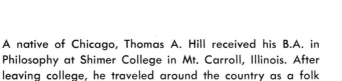

A native of Chicago, Thomas A. Hill received his B.A. in Philosophy at Shimer College in Mt. Carroll, Illinois. After leaving college, he traveled around the country as a folk singer for a year.

In addition to being a folk singer and guitarist, Tom Hill has at one time or another been a marine insurance claims examiner, a magazine writer, a farmhand, a photographer's assistant, a caddy, a cabinet maker, and owner of his own candle-making business. Author of *The Guitar*, another Keynote Book, Tom Hill now resides in Brandon, Vermont, where he writes from a room overlooking a pine forest and a lake.